Pebble™ Plus

Bugs, Bugs, Bugs!

Fireflies

by Margaret Hall

Consulting Editor: Gail Saunders-Smith, PhD
Consultant: Laura Jesse, Extension Associate
Department of Entomology
Iowa State University
Ames, Iowa

Capstone
press

Mankato, Minnesota

Pebble Plus is published by Capstone Press,
151 Good Counsel Drive, P.O. Box 669, Mankato, Minnesota 56002.
www.capstonepress.com

1 2 3 4 5 6 10 09 08 07 06 05

Library of Congress Cataloging-in-Publication Data
Hall, Margaret, 1947–
    Fireflies / by Margaret Hall.
    p. cm.—(Pebble Plus. Bugs, bugs, bugs!)
    Includes bibliographical references and index.
    ISBN-13: 978-0-7368-4253-2 (hardcover)
    ISBN-10: 0-7368-4253-5 (hardcover)
    ISBN-13: 978-0-7368-6126-7 (softcover pbk.)
    ISBN-10: 0-7368-6126-2 (softcover pbk.)
    1. Fireflies—Juvenile literature. I. Title.
QL596.L28H35 2006
595.76'44—dc22   2004029487

Summary: Simple text and photographs describe the physical characteristics of fireflies.

Editorial Credits
Heather Adamson, editor; Linda Clavel, set designer; Ted Williams, book designer; Jo Miller, photo researcher;
    Scott Thoms, photo editor

Photo Credits
Bill Johnson, 5, 21
Brand X Pictures, back cover
Bruce Coleman Inc./John Burnley, 11; E. R. Degginger, 17
Dwight R. Kuhn, front cover, 15
Photo Researchers Inc./Darwin Dale, 1; MacroWorld/Noah Poritz, 13; Stephen Dalton, 19
Unicorn Stock Photos/James Anderson, 9
Visuals Unlimited/Jeff Daly, 7

Note to Parents and Teachers

The Bugs, Bugs, Bugs! set supports national science standards related to the diversity of
life and heredity. This book describes and illustrates fireflies. The images support early
readers in understanding the text. The repetition of words and phrases helps early
readers learn new words. This book also introduces early readers to subject-specific
vocabulary words, which are defined in the Glossary section. Early readers may need
assistance to read some words and to use the Table of Contents, Glossary, Read More,
Internet Sites, and Index sections of the book.

Table of Contents

What Are Fireflies?

Fireflies are small beetles.

Beetles are insects.

Some people call fireflies

lightning bugs.

How Fireflies Look

Most fireflies have
black or brown bodies.
Some fireflies have
yellow, orange, or red marks.

7

Most fireflies are
about the size
of an adult's fingernail.

9

Fireflies have four wings.

Two soft wings
are used to fly.

Two harder wings cover
the soft wings.

11

Fireflies have two antennas.

Fireflies use antennas

to feel and smell.

antenna

What Fireflies Do

The back part
of a firefly's body lights up.
Each kind of firefly
has its own flash.

15

Male and female fireflies

use their lights

to find each other.

Then they mate.

Females lay eggs.

Young fireflies
hatch from eggs.
They are called glowworms.
Their long bodies glow.

19

Glowworms live underground in winter. In spring, they become adults with wings. They crawl out of the dirt and fly away.

21

Glossary

antenna—a feeler; insects use antennas to sense movement, to smell, and to listen to each other.

female—an animal that can give birth to young animals or lay eggs

flash—to turn on and off over and over again

glow—to shine with a soft light

insect—a small animal with a hard outer shell, six legs, three body sections, and two antennas; most insects have wings.

male—an animal that can father young

Read More

Ashley, Susan. *Fireflies*. Let's Read about Insects. Milwaukee: Weekly Reader Early Learning Library, 2004.

Loewen, Nancy. *Living Lights: Fireflies in Your Backyard*. Backyard Bugs. Minneapolis: Picture Window Books, 2004.

St. Pierre, Stephanie. *Firefly*. Bug Books. Chicago: Heinemann, 2002.

Internet Sites

FactHound offers a safe, fun way to find Internet sites related to this book. All of the sites on FactHound have been researched by our staff.

Here's how:

1. Visit *www.facthound.com*

2. Type in this special code **0736842535** for age-appropriate sites. Or enter a search word related to this book for a more general search.

3. Click on the **Fetch It** button.

FactHound will fetch the best sites for you!

Index

Word Count: 135
Grade: 1
Early-Intervention Level: 14